WHAT'S THE GOOD WORD?

WHAT'S THE GOOD WORD?

The All New Super Incredible Bible Study Book for Junior Highs

JOHN C. SOUTER
Illustrated by Tim Bowers

ZONDERVAN PUBLISHING HOUSE
of The Zondervan Corporation • Grand Rapids, Michigan

WHAT'S THE GOOD WORD?

Designed by Martha Bentley
Edited by James E. Ruark

Library of Congress Cataloging in Publication Data

Souter, John C.
What's the good word?

Summary: A textbook for studying the Bible using puzzles, games, and creative activities designed to make the stories of the Bible timely and alive.

1. Bible—Text-books. [1. Bible—Study] I. Bowers, Tim, ill. II. Title.

BS605.2.S68 1983 220.6 83-1274
ISBN 0-310-45891-9

Printed in the United States of America

83 84 85 86 87 88 / 10 9 8 7 6 5 4 3 2

HEY!

THE BIBLE IS EXCITING!

You've never read a book
that has more to tell you
than the Bible—
because there isn't another book like it
anywhere!

God wrote the Bible,
and that's why it's so different.
It is packed full of all kinds
of interesting information.
This book, *What's the Good Word?*,
was written to help you
get the most out of the Bible—
to show you how exciting God's Word can be.

To help you really get the most
out of the Bible,
we recommend that you obtain a copy of
The New International Version.
It is easy to read and understand.
The studies in this book
are based on that Bible,
so you'll want to use it when doing these studies.
A few quotations from Scripture, however,
are from *The Living Bible.*

Contents

Why Study the Bible? Because It Will Help You Be

THE WISEST KID ON THE BLOCK

Why is Waldo J. Ardhammer so amazing?

Why does Wanda Wondergirl stand out in a crowd?

Waldo and Wanda have learned that true wisdom comes from God's Book, the Bible. The more you study it, the wiser you will become. Psalm 119:98–100 says God's Word will make you wiser than your enemies, your teachers, and even those old adults!

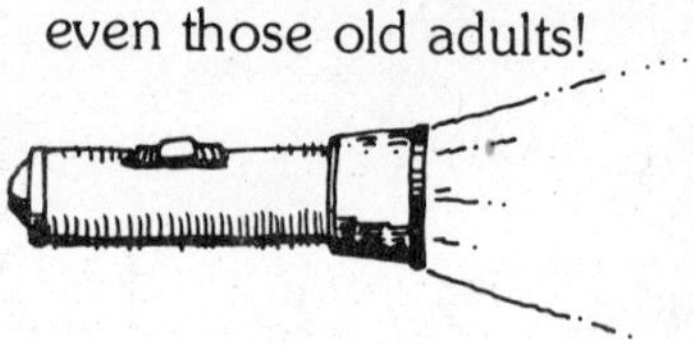

"Your words are a flashlight to light the path ahead of me, and keep me from stumbling."

—Psalm 119:105, TLB

Why Study the Bible? Because It's Interesting.

DID YOU KNOW?

THE BIBLE said the world was hanging in space when most people still believed it was *FLAT.*

Job 26:7

A DONKEY SPOKE to a false prophet named Balaam and told him off.

Numbers 22:20–41

SAMSON killed 1,000 Philistines with the jawbone of a donkey.

Judges 15:8–17

JESUS predicted people would respond to His salvation in one of four ways. Which one are you?

Hard Soil?
Rocky Ground?
Thorny Soil?
Good Ground?

See Mark 4:1–20.

WHO IS REALLY GOD?

Elijah proved it once and for all on Mount Carmel.

2 Kings 18:22–39

ARE YOU IN LOVE?

The greatest passage ever written about love is found in

I Corinthians 13

HOW THE WORLD WILL END!

See the Book of Revelation.

WHAT'S THE BIBLE ALL ABOUT?

God wanted to tell us about himself. He wanted to show us how to live. He also wanted to forgive us for all our sin. That's why he had the Bible written. It is his Instruction Book, as our Creator, for us to follow and obey.

The Bible really isn't just one book—it is a collection of many books. All these books were gathered together into a sort of library. This was divided into two sections, the Old and the New Testaments.

The Old Testament deals with the history of God's chosen people, the Jews. It talks about their nation (Israel) and their problems with unbelief. They rejected God, even though he had sent his Son to open a way into his presence. When they rejected God's Son, Christianity became open to all of us.

The New Testament includes the establishment of Jesus' church and several books on how to live the Christian life. The first four books, called the Gospels, tell us what we need to know about Jesus' life and teachings.

Most of our information about our beliefs comes from the New Testament. But the Old Testament is like the foundation for the rest of the Bible. We need to know what the Old Testament teaches, because without it we won't be able to understand the New Testament clearly.

SUBSCRIBE TODAY
TO THE BOOK OF BOOKS . . .

The BIBLE!

Guaranteed to Change Your Whole Life!

HOW TO USE THIS BOOK

This book has 16 sections or chapters. In each section you will find many different studies to help you get the most out of the Bible. Don't feel you have to study through this book from the front to the back. Feel free to skip around and use whatever study you wish. The important thing is to get into God's Word—the Bible—on a regular basis.

So turn the page and enjoy yourself. Dig deeply into God's Book and learn all about how to please Him.

ONE

Bible Marathon

Marathon runners know how to pace themselves. They don't try to run too far too fast or too soon. So when you do a study of a complete Bible book, you will want to take your time and study it bit by bit.

Ever study your way through an entire Bible book? Probably not. That's what "Bible Marathon" is all about. Use the following pages to study your way through three complete Bible books: James, Ruth, and Mark. Each of the books has been broken up into small pieces based on *The New International Version.* Tell what you find in each paragraph or chapter in your own words.

What Does It Say?

1:1 ______________________________

1:2–8 ______________________________

1:9–11 ______________________________

1:12 ______________________________

1:13–15 ______________________________

1:16–18 ______________________________

1:19–21 ______________________________

1:22–25 ______________________________

1:26–27 ______________________________

2:1–4 ______________________________

2:5–7 ______________________________

2:8–11 ______________________________

2:12–13 ______________________________

2:14–17 ______________________________

2:18–19 ______________________________

2:20–24 ______________________________

2:25–26 ______________________________

JAMES What Does It Say?

3:1–2 ____________________
3:3–6 ____________________
3:7–8 ____________________
3:9–12 ____________________
3:13–16 ____________________
3:17–18 ____________________
4:1–3 ____________________
4:4–6 ____________________
4:7–10 ____________________
4:11–12 ____________________
4:13–17 ____________________
5:1–6 ____________________
5:7–9 ____________________
5:10–11 ____________________
5:12 ____________________
5:13–16 ____________________
5:17–18 ____________________
5:19–20 ____________________

THE BOOK OF RUTH

State in one sentence what happens in each of the 4 chapters of the Book of Ruth.

1 ______________________________

2 ______________________________

3 ______________________________

4 ______________________________

THE BOOK OF MARK

State in one sentence what happens in each of the 16 chapters of the Book of Mark.

1 ______________________________

2 ______________________________

3 ______________________________

4 ______________________________

5 ______________________________

6 ______________________________

7 ______________________________

8 ______________________________

9 ______________________________

10 ______________________________

11 ______________________________

12 ______________________________

13 ______________________________

14 ______________________________

15 ______________________________

16 ______________________________

TWO

Law School

Everybody knows what laws are: "Don't Speed," "Keep off the Grass," "No Smoking." But did you know that there are four Bible books which contain God's laws?

Let's go to Law School and learn what some of these laws are all about. In the following exercise, match the law with the correct verse reference.

THE LAWS	THE REFERENCES
A. Don't Eat Animals Already Dead	____ 1. Leviticus 17:15–16
B. Don't Harvest Every Last Bit; Save Some for the Poor	____ 2. Deuteronomy 12:2–3
C. Don't Falsely Accuse Your Neighbor	____ 3. Leviticus 19:16
D. Don't Curse Your Parents	____ 4. Leviticus 19:9–10
E. Kidnappers Must Die	____ 5. Leviticus 20:9
F. Never Sacrifice a Sickly Ox	____ 6. Deuteronomy 17:1
G. Destroy All the Heathen Altars	____ 7. Exodus 21:16

ON TRIAL

You are about to read actual court records—never before revealed in this way. The cases from both the prosecution and defense have been summarized. You be the jury. You decide whether the defendants are guilty or innocent.

DEFENDANT: **Daniel of Babylon**
OCCUPATION: President
CHARGE: Breaking the law of the Medes and Persians.
COURT DATE: 538 B.C.
LAW: Daniel 6:1–9
EVIDENCE: Daniel 6:10–28
ARGUMENTS FOR THE PROSECUTION:
- This man has broken the law of King Darius.
- This man prayed to his God in violation of the law.
- We've seen him pray with our own eyes.

ARGUMENTS FOR THE DEFENSE:
- There is only one God, and I pray to him.

- Any law stopping a man from praying to God is illegal, because God is really in charge.
- I will willingly disobey all such laws.

Your Verdict: ______________________________

DEFENDANT: **Jesus of Nazareth**
OCCUPATION: Itinerant Preacher/Prophet
CHARGE: Breaking the Sabbath
COURT DATE: A.D. 29
LAW: Exodus 20:8–11; 23:12
EVIDENCE: Matthew 12:1–16
ARGUMENTS FOR THE PROSECUTION:

- This man breaks the Sabbath, and so do his disciples.
- The law says we are not to work on the Sabbath.
- The Pharisees say that to work on the Sabbath is to sin.
- This man heals on the Sabbath and thus breaks the law.

ARGUMENTS FOR THE DEFENSE:

- King David and his men broke the law, and God didn't punish them (1 Samuel 21:1–6).
- "I am greater than the law and the temple, and therefore I can break the Sabbath."
- Healing is the work of God and can therefore be done on any day.
- Man wasn't made for the benefit of the Sabbath.
- The Sabbath was made for man's benefit—to help him rest.

Your Verdict: ______________________________

DEFENDANT: **Anonymous**
OCCUPATION: Unemployed/Harlot
CHARGE: Adultery
COURT DATE: Somewhere near A.D. 28

LAW: Exodus 20:14; Leviticus 20:10
EVIDENCE: John 8:1–11

ARGUMENTS FOR THE PROSECUTION:
- Adultery is wrong.
- This woman was caught in the very act of adultery.
- There can be no doubt about this woman's guilt.
- Moses commanded in the law that such women should be put to death.

ARGUMENTS FOR THE DEFENSE:
- You know yourselves that we are not allowed by the Romans to keep this law today.
- Is there anyone here who has not thought lust in his or her heart?
- "Those who have never sinned can throw the first stones."
- God offers forgiveness to those who have sinned if they repent.

Your Verdict: ______________________________

DEFENDANT: **Saul of Tarsus,** *alias* **Paul**
OCCUPATION: Tentmaker/Pharisee
CHARGE: Murder
COURT DATE: About A.D. 60
LAW: Exodus 20:13; 21:12
EYEWITNESS ACCOUNTS: Acts 7:57–60; 8:3
PERSONAL CONFESSIONS: Galatians 1:13–14; Acts 22:4–5; 26:9–11

ARGUMENTS FOR THE PROSECUTION:
- Murder is wrong.
- The penalty for murder is death.
- Saul admitted that he had been responsible for the death of Christians, even Stephen.
- Saul should die.

ARGUMENTS FOR THE DEFENSE:

- The penalty for murder is death, but God does not always ask for the death penalty.
- Moses murdered and was allowed to live (Exodus 2:11–21).
- David murdered and was allowed to live (2 Samuel 11:14–17; 12:13–14).
- God came to Saul, convicted him, and allowed him to repent.
- Saul's confessions prove how repentant he was; he suffered enough.
- There is forgiveness for murder if there is true repentance.

Your Verdict: ______________________________

THE LAW—ON TRIAL

The Old Testament laws were given so that we could understand how holy and righteous God is—so that we could learn his moral standards.

The thing that is so ironic is that no one keeps them! That's right! No one in all the world can keep God's laws—we're all just too weak. Let's study how God has changed some of these laws, and why he gave them in the first place.

THE OLD LAW		**THE NEW LAW**
Exodus 20:14	Adultery	Matthew 5:27–28

1. Is the old law done away with? ______________________
2. What changes are made? ______________________

THE OLD LAW		**THE NEW LAW**
Exodus 20:13	Murder	Matthew 5:21–22

1. Is the old law done away with? ______________________
2. What changes are made? ______________________

THE OLD LAW — **THE NEW LAW**

Deuteronomy 24:1 — Divorce — Matthew 5:31–32

1. Is the old law done away with? ______________________
2. What changes are made? ______________________

THE OLD LAW — **THE NEW LAW**

Exodus 21:22–25 — Revenge — Matthew 5:38–42

1. Is the old law done away with? ______________________
2. What changes are made? ______________________

WHY WAS THE LAW GIVEN?

Match the quotes with the correct verses below:

A. "Is the law sin? Certainly not! Indeed I would not have known what sin was except through the law."	☐1. Matthew 5:17
B. "So the law was put in charge to lead us to Christ that we might be justified by faith. Now that faith has come, we are no longer under the supervision of the law."	☐2. Romans 7:7
C. "Do not think that I have come to abolish the Law or the Prophets; I have not come to abolish them but to fulfill them."	☐3. Galatians 3:24–25

THREE

Get Smart!

If you've never read the Book of Proverbs, you've missed an exciting experience. Proverbs is full of practical wisdom that you can use in your everyday life. This section is designed to help you get the most out of this interesting Bible book.

Finish These Proverbs:

1. (Proverbs 27:2) "Let another praise you, ________________________________."

2. (Proverbs 23:12) "Apply your heart to instruction ________________________________."

Proverbs-in-a-Box

Write out what the proverb says for each cartoon.

◀Proverbs 10:10

Proverbs 11:22 ▶

◀ Proverbs 19:15

A New Testament proverb:

Matthew 19:24 ▶

Proverbs 5:22

Proverbs 10:19

Draw-Your-Own-Proverb

Below, illustrate each of the proverbs after looking up the passage in *The Living Bible:*

Proverbs 10:8

Proverbs 28:1

Proverbs 10:14

Proverbs 12:5

▲ Proverbs 22:13

▲ Proverbs 27:19

Dial-a-Proverb

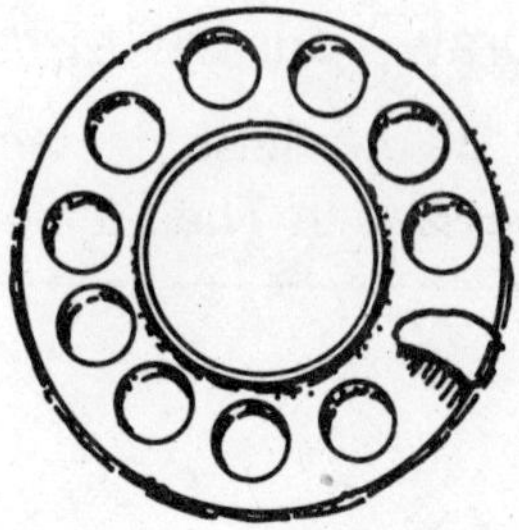

Look up the following Proverbs references and match them with the correct passages below from *The New International Version:*

A. Proverbs 26:28	1. "Better a poor man whose walk is blameless than a rich man whose ways are perverse."
B. Proverbs 11:20	2. "Blessed are those who are persecuted because of righteousness, for theirs is the kingdom of heaven."
C. Proverbs 28:6	3. "A lying tongue hates those it hurts, and a flattering mouth works ruin."
D. Proverbs 3:5–6	4. "Do you see a man skilled in his work? He will serve before kings."

E. Matthew 5:10

F. Proverbs 22:29

5. "The LORD detests men of perverse heart but he delights in those whose ways are blameless."

6. "Trust in the LORD with all your heart and lean not on your own understanding; in all your ways acknowledge him, and he will make your paths straight."

FOUR

The Jukebox

The Bible has its own book of music. Most people don't realize it, but the Book of Psalms is a book of lyrics—poetry that was originally sung to the Lord. Look into the Bible Jukebox and see if you can get to know the Bible tunes.

Name That Tune!

Match the records below with their record jackets. Look up the references and then draw lines between the correct albums and records.

Praise-a-Long

Read the following psalms. Let them give you ideas about how to praise the Lord. After reading each, write your own psalm praise to God. Tell the Lord exactly how you feel about him.

Psalm 27:1–7

Your Psalm: ______________________________

____

____

____

____

____

Psalm 34:1–10

Your Psalm: ______________________________

____

____

____

____

____

Psalm 37:1–7

Your Psalm: ______________________________

____

____

____

____

____

Psalm 139:1-23
Your Psalm: ______________________________

____

____

____

____

____

Psalm 148:1-14
Your Psalm: ______________________________

____

____

____

____

____

FIVE

The Time Machine

Take a ride in the Time Machine. Travel into the past and see what God predicted would happen through his prophets and what predictions he has fulfilled already. Through the Time Machine we can also look into the future to see what God is going to do. Enjoy your journey through time!

Fill in the missing blanks on the Time Machine Report Forms below. Look up the Bible passages and write down what they say.

THE TIME MACHINE REPORT FORM

PROPHET: Jesus of Nazareth

PREDICTION

Date: A.D. 29

Bible Passage: Matthew 24:1–2; Luke 21:20–24

Details: Jesus predicted five things would happen. See if you can find them in above passages.

1. ______________________________
2. ______________________________
3. ______________________________
4. ______________________________
5. ______________________________

FULFILLMENT

Date: A.D. 70

Bible Passage: None

Details: Here is the literal fulfillment of the five things Jesus predicted:

1. Massive temple complex was completely destroyed by Roman general Titus in A.D. 70. Not one stone left upon another.
2. Jerusalem was surrounded by Roman armies in A.D. 69–70.
3. Palestine became a wasteland from A.D. 70 to the twentieth century.
4. The Jews have been persecuted beyond comprehension.
5. Jerusalem and the temple site remained in Gentile hands for 1,900 years until A.D. 1967.

THE TIME MACHINE REPORT FORM

PROPHET: Daniel

PREDICTION

Date: 603 B.C.

Bible Passage: Daniel 2: 27–49

Details: Summarize the passage.

____

____

____

____

____

____

____

FULFILLMENT

Date: 603 B.C. to A.D. 476

Bible Passage: None

Details: Nebuchadnezzar's dream told of four empires. These were the following four empires after Daniel's time.

1. Babylonian Empire (Daniel's time)
2. Medo-Persian Empire
3. Greek Empire
4. Roman Empire

THE TIME MACHINE REPORT FORM

PROPHET: Paul the Apostle

PREDICTION

Date: A.D. 51

Bible Passage: 1 Thessalonians 4:13–18

Details: Summarize the passage.

____

____

____

____

FULFILLMENT

Date: Soon

Bible Passage: None

Details: Not yet fulfilled.

TIME MACHINE CAPSULES

Look into the Time Machine to see the accuracy of Bible predictions about the first coming of God the Son (Jesus) to earth. Look up the passages to confirm that the prophecies were fulfilled, and summarize these under the "Details" part of the form.

PROPHECY NO. 1

PREDICTION

Date: 700 B.C.

Approx. Passage: Micah 5:2

What Was Predicted:
The Messiah's place of birth

FULFILLMENT

Date: 4 to 6 B.C.

Approx. Passage: Matthew 2:1; Luke 2:1–7

Details: ______

PROPHECY NO. 2

PREDICTION

Approx. Date: 730 B.C.

Passage: Isaiah 7:14

What Was Predicted:
Type of birth

FULFILLMENT

Approx. Date: 4 to 6 B.C.

Passage: Matthew 1:18–25

Details: ______

PROPHECY NO. 3

PREDICTION

Approx. Date: 715 B.C.

Passage: Isaiah 53:7

What Was Predicted:
Silent before his accusers

FULFILLMENT

Approx. Date: A.D. 29

Passage: Matthew 27:12–14

Details: ______

PROPHECY NO. 4

PREDICTION

Approx. Date: 1000 B.C.

Passage: Psalm 22:14–18

What Was Predicted:
Method of Messiah's death

Details: ______

FULFILLMENT

Approx. Date: A.D. 29

Passage: John 19:29; 20:25; Luke 23:27, 34–35

Details: ______

SIX

The Headlines

There are many "history books" in the Bible. These books tell the story of God's people from Creation (in Genesis) all the way to the beginning of the church (in the Book of Acts). Bible history is filled with all sorts of exciting stories; it gives us background for other books in the Bible, helping us to see the "big picture" about the people, places, and reasons behind God's actions.

Let's look at Bible history from a newspaper reporter's viewpoint. What headlines and articles would you have written if you had been alive in Bible times?

The Headline Writer

At the news desk of any daily newspaper, the job of an editor is to read the stories, decide which are the most important, then write the headlines. For each of the Bible stories/passages below, there are some suggested headlines. You be the editor. Read the stories as found in the Bible and select the best headline—or write one of your own.

Two rules for writing headlines are (1) Keep them brief, using simple words where possible; and (2) Avoid unnecessary words (such as *the*).

A special challenge: The various tones of the headlines below suggest that different people might have written them. Some are "nasty," others are not. Where the headlines vary in tone, try to figure out on whose "side" each headline writer might be.

1. The Story: John 9

BLIND MAN HEALED,
CAST OUT OF SYNAGOGUE

JESUS HEALS MAN BORN
BLIND; PARENTS QUIET

PHARISEES CAST BLIND
MAN FROM SYNAGOGUE

2. The Story: Acts 21:26–40

FORMER PHARISEE
MOBBED AT TEMPLE

ROMAN SOLDIERS SAVE
JEW FROM ANGRY MOB

APOSTLE PAUL ANGERS
FELLOW JEWS, IS ARRESTED

FAMOUS CHRISTIAN PROFANES
TEMPLE; SAVED BY ROMANS

3. The Story: Acts 9:36–42

DORCAS CLAIMS APOSTLE RAISED HER BACK TO LIFE

PETER FAKES RAISING GIRL FROM DEAD

CRAZY CHRISTIANS RAISE DEAD AGAIN

The Story Writer

Read the following Bible stories and write the opening paragraph—the "lead" paragraph—for each suggested headline below. Remember, the lead paragraph should contain for the newspaper reader the "who, what, when, where," and possibly the "why" of the story.

1. Read the Book of Philemon.

SLAVE RETURNS ON HIS OWN,
CLAIMS TO BE CHRISTIAN

It was reported today that Onesimus, a former slave, . . .

2. Read Hosea 1.

PROPHET WEDS PROSTITUTE,
CLAIMS SHE'S LIKE ISRAEL

3. Read Matthew 2:1–18.

HEROD ENRAGED, SLAYS
BABIES IN BETHLEHEM

4. Read Joshua 2.

SPIES HOME, SAFE;
CLOSE CALL IN JERICHO

SEVEN

The Telegrams

Prayers are like telegrams. They go straight to their destination without delay. They are telegraphed right to the One who can answer them in a hurry. Here are some famous prayers from the Bible.

TELEGRAM

LORD, STOP IT FROM RAINING!

—See 1 Kings 17:1–9 for the results.

TELEGRAM

"O LORD MY GOD, HAVE YOU BROUGHT TRAGEDY UPON THIS WIDOW I AM STAYING WITH, BY CAUSING HER SON TO DIE? . . . O LORD MY GOD, LET THIS BOY'S LIFE RETURN TO HIM!"

—See 1 Kings 17:10–24 for the results.

TELEGRAM

"O LORD, GOD OF ABRAHAM, ISAAC AND ISRAEL, LET IT BE KNOWN TODAY THAT YOU ARE GOD IN ISRAEL AND THAT I AM YOUR SERVANT AND HAVE DONE ALL THESE THINGS AT YOUR COMMAND. ANSWER ME, O LORD, ANSWER ME, SO THESE PEOPLE WILL KNOW THAT YOU, O LORD, ARE GOD, AND THAT YOU ARE TURNING THEIR HEARTS BACK AGAIN."

—See 1 Kings 18:1–45 for the results.

We can be thankful that God doesn't always answer our prayers the way we ask him to. If he did, we'd sometimes be in trouble! Here's a prayer-telegram Elijah sent off to God, but which did not receive a "yes" answer.

TELEGRAM

"I HAVE HAD ENOUGH, LORD. TAKE MY LIFE; I AM NO BETTER THAN MY ANCESTORS."

—Read 1 Kings 19:1–21 for the results.

Here's a prayer-telegram that went up to God when Peter was put into prison by Herod. The early church prayed this basic prayer.

TELEGRAM

LORD, WE EARNESTLY PRAY FOR PETER, ASKING YOU TO PROTECT HIM FROM HEROD AND FREE HIM.

—See Acts 12:1–24 for the results.

What Are Your Prayer Requests?

It is important when we pray that we ask for things that are according to God's will. If we ask selfishly for riches and things like becoming the most beautiful or popular person in school—the chances are very good God knows these things are not in our best interests and he won't give them to us. So we must make sure we ask for things that we know the Lord wants us to have.

Dates

My Needs ______________________________

____

My Family's Needs ______________________________

____

Needs of My Christian Friends ______________________________

____

Needs of My Non-Christian Friends ______________________________

____

The Answers I Have Received ______________________________

____

My Needs ______________________________

____

My Family's Needs ______________________

____

Needs of My Christian Friends ____________

____

Needs of My Non-Christian Friends _________

____

The Answers I Have Received _____________

____

Your Personal Telegrams

Sometimes it is a good idea to write down your prayers. When you tell God what you want to do with your life, he doesn't forget—but you often do. Use the following Telegram Form to write down many of your most important prayers.

PERSONAL **TELEGRAMS** TO GOD

Dates

____

____

____

____

____

____

____

____

____

____

____

____

EIGHT

Bible Ads

Although there were no newspapers (such as we have today) in Israel during the Bible years, we can be certain that businesses and people advertised in different ways. This section is intended to help you see how things could have been if you lived two or three thousand years ago. It should help you to see the Bible in contemporary terms.

CLASSIFIED ADS

FOR SALE

MANURE—All kinds and types. One year's supply. You shovel. Call in person on Mount Ararat. Ask for Ham, Japheth, or Shem. (Read Genesis 6-8.)

LARGE SWORD—For sale. Weight of iron point, 15 pounds. Goliath was last owner. Lost his head. See David, son of Jesse in Philistia. (1 Samuel 17; 21:9.)

FISH AND BREAD—12 baskets of broken pieces. See the disciples at the Sea of Galilee. (Matthew 14:17-21.)

Write a "For Sale" ad for a stretcher (Mark 2:1–12) and for a birthright (Genesis 25:23–34).

PERSONALS

Been charged too much taxes? If you've been defrauded by me—Zacchaeus the tax collector—I will repay you three times what I owe you. This is no joke. I've met Jesus the Prophet from Galilee and my life has been changed. Apply to Tax Office at the city gates, Jericho. (Luke 19:1-10.)

Abinadab, my son, please come home. I know you've received all your inheritance and wasted it, but we still love you. Please come home, the fatted calf is waiting. Dad. (Luke 15:11-32.)

Write your own classified ads for the "Personal" section. Use Luke 15:8–10 to write an ad for a woman looking for a lost coin. Use 2 Samuel 15–18 to write a "Personal" ad from King David to his son Absalom.

HELP WANTED

TENTMAKER'S HELPER needed for aging apostle. Must be willing to work. Must be open to the Gospel. Apply in person. Apostle Paul, 75 Appian Way, Corinth. (Acts 18:1-3.)

SOLDIERS of fortune, rogues, outlaws, and thieves wanted to join army of rebellion against King Saul. Apply with own weapons to the wilderness. See David. (1 Samuel 22:2.)

FISHERMEN needed, for good family fishing business. Sons left business to join the Nazarene. Apply in Capernaum at home of Zebedee, mornings and weekends. (Mark 1:16-20.)

Write a "Help Wanted" ad for Jesus asking for disciples (see Mark 3:13; Luke 9:23–27). Write an ad for King Saul asking for a new harp player (1 Samuel 16:14–23; 18:10–11). Do one for King Solomon asking for more wives (1 Kings 11:1-3).

DISPLAY ADS

Display ads are set up so that a company can better sell its product to the world. Look at the following ads and see if you can create some display ads for yourself.

Second Coming Productions
Proudly Presents

THE RETURN OF THE LORD

Starring: Jesus Christ
Co-Starring: Thousands of Believers
Produced by: The Father
Screenplay by: The Holy Spirit
Special Music by: Michael and the Archangel Choir

Don't Miss This Greatest of All Motion Picture Productions

Release Date: Soon to Be Announced

IN TROUBLE WITH THE LAW?

HAVE you been arrested by the Pharisees, the Sadducees, or the Temple police? If so, you need legal help. That's where we come in. The Legal Aid Society of Jerusalem specializes in handling cases such as yours. We know the law; we're experts in the Ten Commandments and will make certain you don't lose your case. Remember, nobody likes to be stoned, and with our help you won't have to suffer that terrible fate.

Judea Legal Aid Society
606 Malachi Street
Jerusalem, Israel

Would You Like To Have A Body Like Mine?

Who wouldn't! The beautiful body you see above is not just for show. Those muscles have killed thousands of Philistines. They have ripped city gates right out of the walls in which they stood. With muscles like mine you'll never again be pushed around. Learn my secret to a healthier, stronger, more beautiful you. Just send 1,000 shekels to:

SAMSON'S BODY BUILDING COURSE
33 Pumping Iron Road
Gaza, Philistia

Write Your Own Advertisements.

Here is a list of possible customers for your ad-writing services. Choose one client and prepare one ad below:

1. Joseph of Arimathea, selling used tombs (John 19: 38-42).
2. The Egyptian government, for a new Pharaoh (Exodus 14:21–31).
3. King Darius, publicizing the proclamation found in Ezra 5.
4. The king of Aram, concerning a cure for Naaman's leprosy (2 Kings 5).
5. The church in Laodicea, publicizing how wealthy and spiritual its congregation is (Revelation 3:14–22).

NINE

Comic Strips

This section illustrates the Bible in comic-strip form. Look up the Bible passages on which each of the comics is based and follow the instructions.

Read the Book of Jonah.

1. Why do you think Jonah didn't want to go to Nineveh?
2. Why did God have Jonah swallowed by the great fish?
3. What do you think you would have done if you had been in Jonah's situation?

Read Acts 3 and 4: A Healing in the Temple.

Peter and John walk in the temple.

1. Do you think you would have been as fearless as Peter and John?
2. Where did their boldness come from?
3. Why were the temple authorities so upset?

The following comic strips have drawings but no dialogue captions. Read the Scripture passages and try to provide the right dialogue to suit the drawings, then answer the questions below.

Read Genesis 4:1–16: Cain and Abel.

1. Why did God want a sacrifice of an animal? (See Hebrews 9:22.)
2. Why was Cain's sacrifice rejected? (See 1 John 3:12; Hebrews 11:4.)
3. Why did Cain kill his brother? (See 1 John 3:12 again.)

Read Isaiah 38:
Hezekiah's Illness.

1. What would you have done if a prophet said you were going to die?
2. How many years were added to Hezekiah's life?
3. Ten degrees on a sun dial is approximately forty minutes. Why did God add forty minutes to the day?

Here are two comic strips with captions and no pictures. Try to draw your own cartoons to fit the captions. Read the Bible passages carefully so that you will understand the stories fully.

Read Exodus 3 and 4: The Calling of Moses.

Moses! Who is it?	Take off your shoes. I'm the God of your fathers.
I'm going to send you to Pharaoh. I'm not Your man.	I'll be with you. But they won't believe me.
Throw down your rod. Eck!	Anything You say, Lord!

1. Why do you think Moses was so reluctant?
2. How did God win Moses over?

Read Matthew 19:16–22: The Rich Young Ruler.

Good Master,
What must I do to
inherit eternal life?

When you
call me good,
you are
calling
me God.

Keep the
commandments.

Which ones?

Don't kill, commit adultery,
steal, lie. Do honor your
parents, love your
neighbor as yourself.

I've done all these
things. Is there
anything else?

Go and sell every-
thing you have and
give the money to
the poor.

The man went away sad, for he
was very rich.

1. Why did Jesus say, "When you call me good, you are calling me God"?
2. Did the rich man really keep all those commandments?
3. Why did he go away sad?

TEN

The Bible Auto Club

Do you remember the verse that Waldo J. Ardhammer and Wanda Wondergirl provided in the front of this book? (Look up Psalm 119:105 if you forgot.) That is just one verse that tells us how the Bible guides us on the pathway of life. The Bible offers many helps to speed us along our adventure of traveling toward heaven.

Road Signs

It is important that every member of the B.A.C. (Bible Auto Club) know not only the rules of the road, but also the common road signs. Here are some spiritual road signs—verses for you to commit to memory so that your travels will be much easier down the road of life.

Romans 3:23 Romans 6:13 John 10:10b John 14:6 Proverbs 14:12

Auto Club Membership

Like any other auto club, the Bible Auto Club has membership requirements. All you have to do to become a member is to ask Jesus into your heart. Send no money! Jesus has already paid the price in full! Everyone can become a member of the Bible Auto Club (B.A.C. also stands for Born-Again Christian). Just invite Christ into your heart today. Only don't delay, as Jesus may come at any moment and take all true Christians to heaven—and you don't want to be left behind.

BIBLE AUTO CLUB
This is to certify that

____
(Name)
has invited Jesus into his heart
and is now a member of the B.A.C.

____
(Director)

Membership Packet

Now that you are a member of the B.A.C., we would like to give you your official membership packet.

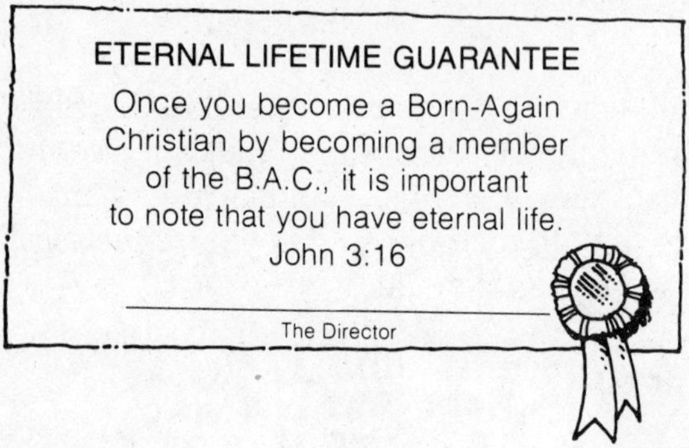

Your road manual for trouble-shooting any problem:

Your pit crew to help you make repairs:

Trip tickets (promises) for the journey ahead of you:

The Road Maps of Life

Your Bible Auto Club provides you with maps to help make your journey along the road of life easier. Psalm 119: 19–20 says: "I am but a pilgrim here on earth: how I need a map—and your commands are my chart and guide. I long for your instructions more than I can tell." Examine the following maps and look up the Bible verses listed on them.

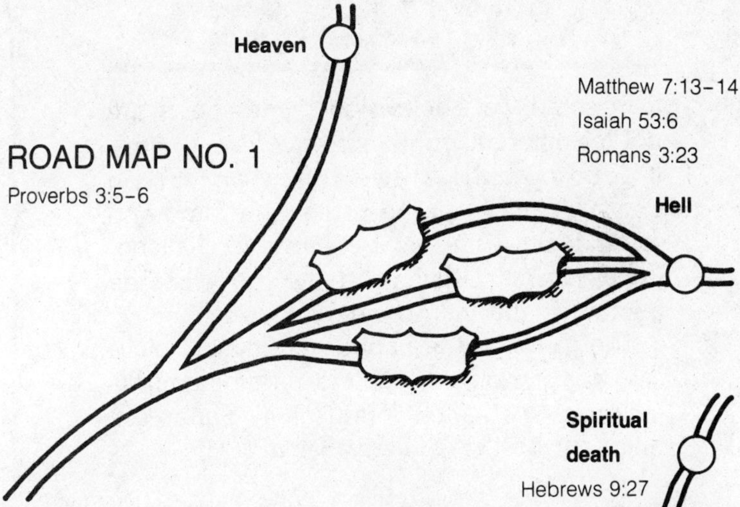

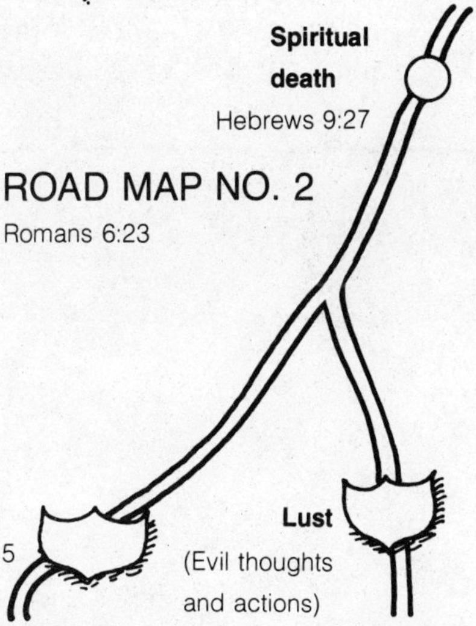

ELEVEN

Jerusalem Squares

In some ways television game shows are not far different from any other kind of quiz. If you know the answers, you win; if you don't . . . there go the prizes and fame and fortune. But with visual effects and challenging electronic variations, game shows can be a lot more fun than ordinary contests.

The game you are about to play is a biblical variation on the age-old pastime of tick-tack-toe. It's called "Jerusalem Squares," and your host is . . . Jerry Salem.

Announcer: "Hello out there in TV land. Today on 'Jerusalem Squares' we have nine noted Bible celebrities who have come to join us. You can play this game with a friend—there at home in front of your TV set—or just play the game by yourself. Choose any square below for your first question. It will be helpful if you can have someone else read the questions to you so you won't be able to get a sneak look at the other questions for the game.

"If you get the question right (you will know by looking up the Bible verse), put an X in the appropriate box. If your answer is wrong, your opponent receives an O in the same box. After you have answered, your friend takes his or her turn. The object of the game is to get three Xs or Os in a row—then you win.

"There are two separate sets of questions for panel one below, enabling you to play two separate games. Mark the Xs and Os in the bottom lefthand corner of a square for the first game and the bottom righthand corner for the second. And now . . . let's play 'Jerusalem Squares'!"

PANEL ONE

All statements are either true or false. Look up the verses to get the correct answers. The Word of God will act as the judge in this game. The judge's decision is final.

Game One

1. Jesus: "You said: 'For God so loved the world, he gave his only Son'" (John 3:16).

2. Paul: "You never actually go to visit Rome" (Acts 28:16).

3. Saul: "You were the first king to rule Israel" (1 Samuel 10:1).

4. Mary: "Joseph was your husband and the father of Jesus" (Matthew 1:18–24).

5. Eve: "After you talked to the serpent in the Garden of Eden, you deliberately sinned" (1 Timothy 2:14).

6. Gideon: "You had 3,000 men with you when you attacked Midian" (Judges 7:7–8).

7. Barnabas: "Your real name is Joseph. 'Barnabas' is just your nickname" (Acts 4:36).

8. Peter: "Your real name is Simon, and you are the son of Jonah" (Matthew 16:17–18).

9. David: "You had Uriah killed after you had committed adultery with his wife" (2 Samuel 12:9).

Game Two

1. Jesus: "You said, 'Blessed are the rich and wealthy, for they shall see God'" (Matthew 19:23).

2. Paul: "You became a believer in Jesus on the road to Tarsus" (Acts 9:1–15).

3. Saul: "You wanted David to become the next king of Israel when you died" (1 Samuel 20:30–31).

4. Mary: "You asked Jesus for help when they ran out of wine at the wedding in Cana" (John 2:3–5).

5. Eve: "Your first son's name was Seth" (Genesis 4:1, 25).

6. Gideon: "You were a very self-confident fighter for the Lord" (Judges 6:36–40).

7. Barnabas: "You had a big argument with the apostle Paul" (Acts 15:36–39).

8. Peter: "You told the Lord you would never deny him" (Mark 14:31).

9. David: "The Lord promised that your kingdom would never end" (2 Samuel 7:12–13).

PANEL TWO

Game Three

1. Joseph: "You were thrown into prison because you committed adultery with Potiphar's wife" (Genesis 39: 7–20).

2. Jesus: "You were surprised when Judas Iscariot betrayed you" (John 13:21–30).

3. Solomon: "You fell away from the Lord at the end of your reign as king" (1 Kings 11:4–8).

4. Delilah: "You cut off Samson's hair" (Judges 16: 18–20).

5. John the Baptist: "You were a cousin of Jesus of Nazareth" (Luke 1:36, 60).

6. Abraham: "You had your first child at age 100" (Genesis 17:17).

7. Isaiah: "You were a godly king in Israel" (Isaiah 1:1).

8. Noah: "You selected two and only two of every animal to go into the ark" (Genesis 7:2).

9. Luke: "You were a Gentile doctor" (Colossians 4:11, 14).

Game Four

1. Joseph: "Your brothers ended up bowing down to you" (Genesis 42:6).

2. Jesus: "You told your disciples exactly when the end of the world was coming" (Acts 1:6–7).

3. Solomon: "You had 700 wives and 300 concubines" (1 Kings 11:1–3).

4. Delilah: "You were a Jewish girl who led Samson astray" (Judges 16:4–5).

5. John the Baptist: "Your diet consisted of wild honey and locusts" (Mark 1:6).

6. Abraham: "After Isaac was born, you had many more children" (Genesis 25:1–3).

7. Isaiah: "You knew you had a dirty mouth" (Isaiah 6:5).

8. Noah: "You had 120 years to build the ark" (Genesis 5:32; 6:3; 7:6).

9. Luke: "You wrote only one Bible book" (Luke 1:1–4; Acts 1:1).

TWELVE

Writing School

Take a short course in writing. Learn to express Bible truths in your own words so that you can apply them more readily to your life.

Fill-in-the-Blanks (Make this personal.)

John 3:16. "For God so loved __________ that he gave his one and only Son, that __________, who believes in him, shall not perish but have eternal life."

Galatians 2:20. "__________ has been crucified with Christ and __________ no longer lives, but Christ lives in __________. The real life __________ lives in the body, __________ lives by faith in the Son of God, who loved __________ and gave himself for __________."

Romans 12:1–2. "Therefore, I urge you, __________, in view of God's mercy, to offer your body as a living sacrifice, holy and pleasing to God—which is your spiritual worship. __________, do not conform any longer to the pattern of this world, but be transformed by the renewing of your mind. Then __________ will be able to test and approve what God's will is—his good, pleasing and perfect will."

In-Your-Own-Words

Read the following Bible passages and put them into your own words:

Romans 2:1–4. ______________________________

____

____

____

____

____

Romans 8:5–8.

1 Corinthians 6:18–20.

James 1:22–25.

THIRTEEN

To Tell The Truth

"Hi, folks, welcome to tonight's edition of 'To Tell the Truth.' As always, this is your game show host Lucifer Serpent—the father of all lies. It's your job to ask the questions of our different contestants and see who's really telling the truth. Remember, all of our contestants will tell the truth sometime—and all will stretch the truth (that means lie) if they don't know the answer. All, that is, except the true Bible character.

"Okay, let's begin with our first set of three guests. What is your name?"

PANEL ONE

"My name is
Saul of Tarsus."

"My name is
Paul the Apostle."

"My name is
Paul."

Question A: "Did you ever commit any crimes in the pursuit of your religious beliefs?"

1. "I am a Hebrew of the Hebrews, a Pharisee of the Pharisees. I would *never* do such a thing."

2. "I must admit that I persecuted the church. I'm very ashamed about it now."

3. "Yes. I did disobey the Law occasionally and I also did persecute Christians."

Question B: "Did you ever get angry with James, the Lord's brother?"

1. "Yes. We parted company on my second missionary journey after an argument over another helper."

2. "No, not to my knowledge."

3. "We had a real falling out. He was being hypocritical and I called him down for it. I didn't care who he was."

Question C: "Do you believe that Jesus is perfect and also God?"

1. "Jesus is certainly perfect. But I wouldn't call Jesus God—he is the Son of God."

2. "Yes, Jesus is perfect. He is also God. I put both of these beliefs in my letters."

3. "Yes, Jesus is perfect and God at the same time. But He should not be considered 'God' in the same sense that the Father is."

Question D: "Do you teach that we should obey authority?"

1. "Obey those in authority only if it is God's will. If it's not God's will, don't obey."

2. "Obey those in authority at all times unless they tell you to do something God says not to do or vice versa."

3. "Yes, obey whatever authority is over you, no matter what they tell you to do."

Lucifer: "Now you have heard from each of the members on our panel. Take a few moments to learn who is right. Look up the following references to see who is really telling the truth."

References: A. Galatians 1:13; B. Galatians 2:11; Acts 15:36–40; C. 2 Corinthians 5:21; Titus 2:13; D. Romans 13:1–2; Acts 5:29.

Who is the real apostle Paul? ____________________

Lucifer: "Now it's time for our second panel of guests. Would you give your names, gentlemen?"

PANEL TWO

"My name is Jeremiah."

"Jeremiah."

"That's my name too—Jeremiah."

Question A: "How many Bible books did you write?"

1. "Two. The Book of Jeremiah, of course, and also the Book of Lamentations."

2. "Only one. The book that bears my name."

3. "Two, to be exact. The Book of Jeremiah and the Book of Ecclesiastes."

Question B: "What was one of the toughest situations you ever got into?"

1. "I guess when I was thrown into a well because I didn't prophesy the way people wanted me to."

2. "Believe me, because I was a prophet of doom, I was in many tough situations. Probably when I was beaten by the mob."

3. "The toughest situation I had to face was when I had to fight against 400 priests of Baal up on Mount Carmel."

Question C: "Were you ever afraid?"

1. "If you want to know the truth, sometimes I was so scared I got upset with the Lord."

2. "I really enjoyed telling people what God was going to do to them if they didn't repent."

3. "I was never afraid because we prophets are made out of strong moral fiber."

Lucifer: "Read a few Scripture passages to decide which guest is telling the truth. Take as much time as you need in order to get to the truth."

References: A. Jeremiah 1:1; Ecclesiastes 1:1; "Lamentations" in a Bible dictionary; B. Jeremiah 37:15–16; 38:6–10; C. Jeremiah 20:7–10, 14–18.

Lucifer: "Now, who is the real prophet Jeremiah: One, two, or three?"

THE MYSTERY GUEST

Lucifer: "And now, folks, it's time for our special mystery guest. Won't you welcome this person with a round of applause? This guest will only tell the truth, but you'll have to guess who it is. Select one question at a time, and write down the name on the right as soon as you know who it is. Keep looking at the questions and answers to make certain you are correct. If you want to guess, go ahead. After you've finished all the questions and answers, look up the true identity of this Bible character, using the references given below.

---

1. Question: "Are you found in the Old Testament?"
   Answer: "No."
2. Question: "Are you found in the New Testament?"
   Answer: "Yes."
3. Question: "Are you a male?"
   Answer: "Yes."
4. Question: "Are you a resident of Galilee?"
   Answer: "Yes."
5. Question: "Are you named in the Letters or Revelation?"
   Answer: "No."
6. Question: "Are you named in the Gospels?"
   Answer: "Yes."
7. Question: "Are you a 'good guy'?"
   Answer: "Yes."
8. Question: "Did you walk with Jesus?"
   Answer: "Yes."
9. Question: "Were you one of the twelve disciples?"
   Answer: "Yes."
10. Question: "Was your father's name Jonas?
    Answer: "Yes."
11. Question: "Was your trade that of fisherman?"
    Answer: "Yes."
12. Question: "Were you a follower of John the Baptist?"
    Answer: "Yes."

13. Question: "Did you bring your brother to Jesus?"
Answer: "Yes."

14. Question: "Were you quiet most of the time?"
Answer: "Yes."

15. Question: "Was your brother's name Simon Peter?"
Answer: "Yes."

References: See John 1:44; Mark 1:29; Matthew 4:18–19.

Lucifer: "Who do you think the mystery guest is?"

FOURTEEN

Post Office

The New Testament is composed mostly of letters written from early Christian leaders to first-century churches and new Christians. If there were stamps on the New Testament letters to indicate their destinations, they might have looked like those on the next page. Try to match each city with its correct stamp.

The Stamps

1. Letter to the Romans
2. Letter to the Corinthians
3. Letter to the Ephesians (See Acts 19:23–28.)
4. Letter to Laodicea (See Revelation 3:14–16.)
5. Letter to the Philippians (See Acts 16:11–12.)
6. Letter to the Thessalonians

The Letters

Most New Testament letters were written to answer specific problems. Let's look at some of these problems.

> "To: The Church of Thessalonica,
>
> "Keep away from every brother who is idle and does not live according to the teaching you received from us. . . . 'If a man will not work, he shall not eat.'
>
> "We hear that some among you are idle. They are not busy; they are busybodies."
>
> —2 Thessalonians 3:6, 11

1. How would you have answered this letter? ______________

____

____

____

2. What did Paul tell them to do? (See 2 Thessalonians 3:12.) ____________________

____

____

____

> "To: The Church at Corinth,
>
> "It is actually reported that there is sexual immorality among you, and of a kind that does not occur even among pagans: A man has his father's wife [that is, his stepmother]."
>
> —1 Corinthians 5:1

1. What would you recommend for such a problem in the church? ____________________

____

____

____

2. What did Paul tell them to do? (See 1 Corinthians 5:2–13.) ____________________

____

____

> "To: The Galatians,
>
> "You foolish Galatians! Who has bewitched you? . . . I would like to learn one thing from you: Did you receive the Spirit by observing the law, or by believing what you heard? Are you so foolish? After beginning with the Spirit, are you now trying to attain your goal by human effort?"
>
> —Galatians 3:1–3

The Christians in Galatia had started adding the Old Testament rules and regulations to their belief in Christ because they had been told that it made them better believers. Paul said this was wrong.

1. How would you have answered them? ____________

____

____

2. How did Paul answer? (See Galatians 3:5, 23–25.) ___

____

____

____

The Heavy Stuff

Most of the New Testament letters contain basic teaching about our relationship with God. We would call this the "heavy stuff"—or the doctrines of Christianity.

In the Bible passages quoted below there are many basic teachings. See how many of the doctrines listed below you can find taught in these passages. Draw lines between the doctrines and the verse phrases.

Salvation = "Having our sin taken away"

Faith = "Simply trusting God"

Grace = "Unmerited favor or blessing"

Justification = "Just as if we had never sinned"

"Now all praise to God for his wonderful kindness to us and his favor that he has poured out upon us, because we belong to his dearly loved Son. So overflowing is his kindness towards us that he took away all our sins through the blood of his Son, by whom we are saved; and he has showered down upon us the richness of his grace—for how well he understands us and knows what is best for us at all times" (Ephesians 1:6–8).

"Because of his kindness you have been saved through trusting Christ. And even trusting is not of yourselves; it too is a gift from God. Salvation is not a reward for the good we have done, so none of us can take any credit for it" (Ephesians 2:8–9).

FIFTEEN

Bible Puzzle Section

This section has a variety of codes and puzzles drawn from many portions of Scripture, including both the Old Testament and the New. You'll find some familiar puzzle forms and perhaps some intriguing new ones. If you make it to the end without getting stumped, go to the head of the class.

Crack the Codes

1. The following code is for a Bible verse. Every number represents a letter. The words are found in Matthew 28:19 in *The New International Version.*

__ __   __ __ __   __ __ __ __
7 15   1 14 4   13 1 11 5

4 9 19 3 9 16 12 5 19

15 6   1 12 12

14 1 20 9 15 14 19

2. Here's another puzzle using the above code. The words are found in Philippians 4:4. See if you can fill in the letters without looking up the verse.

18 5 10 15 9 3 5   9 14

20 8 5   12 15 18 4

1 12 23 1 25 19

3. Here's a new code, similar to the last one, but each number represents a different letter than it did in the last code. This time the words are found in 1 John 2:15.

23 12   13 12 7   15 12 5 22

7 19 22   4 12 9 15 23

4. Same code as number 3 above. This time the words are found in 1 Corinthians 13:4.

$\overline{15}$ $\overline{12}$ $\overline{5}$ $\overline{22}$ $\overline{18}$ $\overline{8}$

$\overline{11}$ $\overline{26}$ $\overline{7}$ $\overline{18}$ $\overline{22}$ $\overline{13}$ $\overline{7}$’

$\overline{15}$ $\overline{12}$ $\overline{5}$ $\overline{22}$ $\overline{18}$ $\overline{8}$

$\overline{16}$ $\overline{18}$ $\overline{13}$ $\overline{23}$

Match-Ups

Match the following titles:

The Lion Tamer	Noah
The Strong Man	Solomon
The Wise King	Samson
The Patient Man	David
The Giant Killer	Daniel
The Sea Captain	Job

If you need some help, the following Scripture passages offer clues: Genesis 6–9; Judges 16; 1 Samuel 17; 1 Kings 3; Job 1–2; Daniel 6.

First Things First

Below is a list of Bible events. See if you can put them in chronological order. Number these from 1 to 10 to show in what sequence they happened.

__ Noah was saved in the ark.
__ Abraham was called by God.
__ Paul preached in Athens.
__ Jesus died on the cross.
__ God created the world.
__ Stephen was stoned to death.
__ Moses parted the Red Sea.
__ David killed Goliath.
__ Jesus turned water to wine.
__ John the Baptist was born.

If you're stumped, check these Bible references: Genesis 1; 8; 12; Exodus 14; 1 Samuel 17; Luke 1; John 2; 19; Acts 7; 17.

Your Menu

In Leviticus 11:1–47 several animals are listed as being "unclean." Rules were also given to the Jews so they could know which animals were clean even if they weren't listed by name. Some of these rules had health reasons (although their primary purpose was to teach the people about God and how to live for God—see verses 44–46), and these helped the people of Israel avoid diseases and physical problems which we understand today.

Which of the following animals do you think you would be allowed to eat under these rules? Circle your answers.

lobster	clams	pig	mouse	grasshopper
crab	weasel	swan	bat	antelope
locust	hare	cow	lizard	beetle

Which animals do you think you *would* have eaten? _____

____

The Parable Problem

See if you can match the following list of parables with their basic teaching. If you can't, look up the references.

Good Samaritan (Luke 10:30–35)	The size of our faith.
Lost Sheep (Luke 15:3–7)	The joy of seeing someone come back to the fold.
Mustard Seed (Matthew 13:31)	True neighborliness.

Prodigal Son (Luke 15:11–32)	God gives rewards as He pleases.
Laborers in the Vineyard (Matthew 20:1–16)	The worth of the Gospel.
Friend at Midnight (Luke 11:5–8)	God's love for repentant sinners.
Hidden Treasure (Matthew 13:44)	Effectiveness of persistent prayer.

Find the Words

Search for all the names of God listed below. Look in every direction: frontward, backward, up, and down.

O	T	H	E	W	O	R	D	F	T	Z	U
Y	T	H	G	I	M	L	A	W	D	Y	F
O	N	A	N	R	H	M	D	L	H	R	W
C	J	N	G	G	O	D	O	Q	P	E	X
K	M	O	P	R	L	R	G	C	T	T	M
J	E	S	U	S	Y	D	F	G	Y	R	S
U	S	T	S	A	S	N	O	E	V	O	D
M	S	A	V	E	P	H	N	I	V	F	N
B	I	E	M	U	I	N	O	L	O	M	K
L	A	Z	C	H	R	I	S	T	Q	O	I
P	H	B	I	F	I	B	O	N	I	C	Y
X	W	N	R	O	T	A	E	R	C	V	H

Word List

ALMIGHTY
CHRIST
COMFORTER
CREATOR
DOVE
GOD
HOLY SPIRIT
JESUS
MESSIAH
SON OF GOD
THE WORD

SIXTEEN

The Game of Life

The Game of Life is a board game that can be played either by yourself or with friends. The object of the game is to become a Christian—so that you are saved from your sin. If you "die" or come to the end of the board without becoming a Christian, *you lose.*

INSTRUCTIONS

Equipment

Besides the game board and cards provided in this book, one cube playing die (or a game spinner with numbers 1 to 6) will be needed. Each player must use a token (such as a small coin or a button) as a marker to move about the game board.

The Play

All players begin at START. Roll one die per turn and move ahead by the number of squares indicated on the die. For example, if a player rolls a "4" on the first turn, he or she would advance the token four squares ahead to the space that reads "Age 10." When a player has completed a turn, the player to the left takes a turn, and so on around the circle. A player is finished when he or she either dies or reaches the end of the board. The game is over when the last player is finished. If you have "become a Christian" during the game, you win. If not, you lose. In this game, everyone can be a winner.

Chance Cards

There are a number of Chance Cards provided in this book. These are to be cut out and placed in a pile in the space provided on the board. When you land on a square with CHANCE printed on it, draw one card from the pile of Chance Cards and do exactly what it tells you.

If you are on the CHANCE square indicating your age as 14 and your card tells you to add 12 years to your age, you will look for a square with "Age 26." However, since there is no square with "Age 26," place your token on the "Age 25" square. *If your player age falls between the ages marked on two adjoining squares, as in the example above, always place your token on the square next below your actual game age.*

(Continued on page 90.)

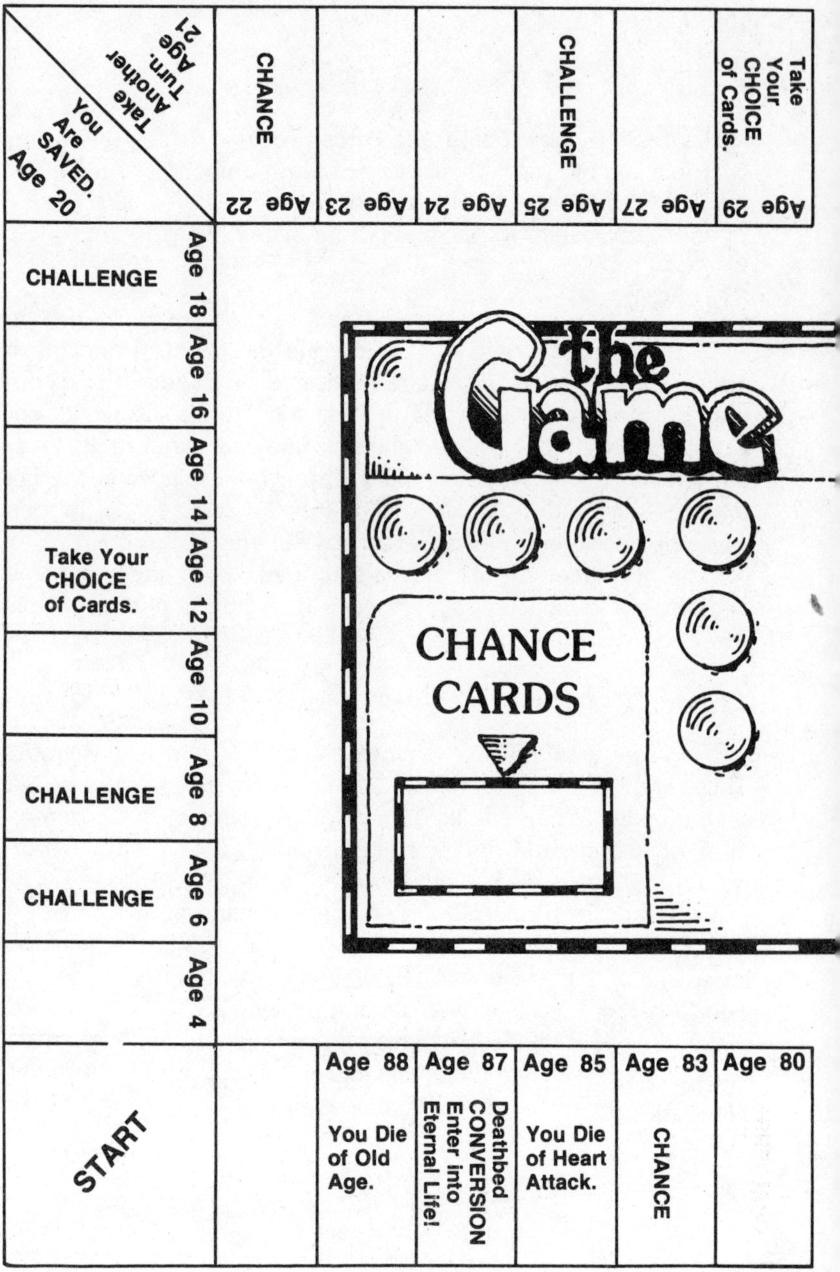
START
Age 4
Age 6
CHALLENGE
Age 8
CHALLENGE
Age 10
Age 12
Take Your CHOICE of Cards.
Age 14
Age 16
Age 18
CHALLENGE
You Are SAVED. Age 20
Take Another Turn. Age 21
Age 22
CHANCE
Age 23
Age 24
Age 25
CHALLENGE
Age 27
Age 29
Take Your CHOICE of Cards.
the Game
CHANCE CARDS
Age 80
Age 83
CHANCE
Age 85
You Die of Heart Attack.
Age 87
Deathbed CONVERSION Enter into Eternal Life!
Age 88
You Die of Old Age.

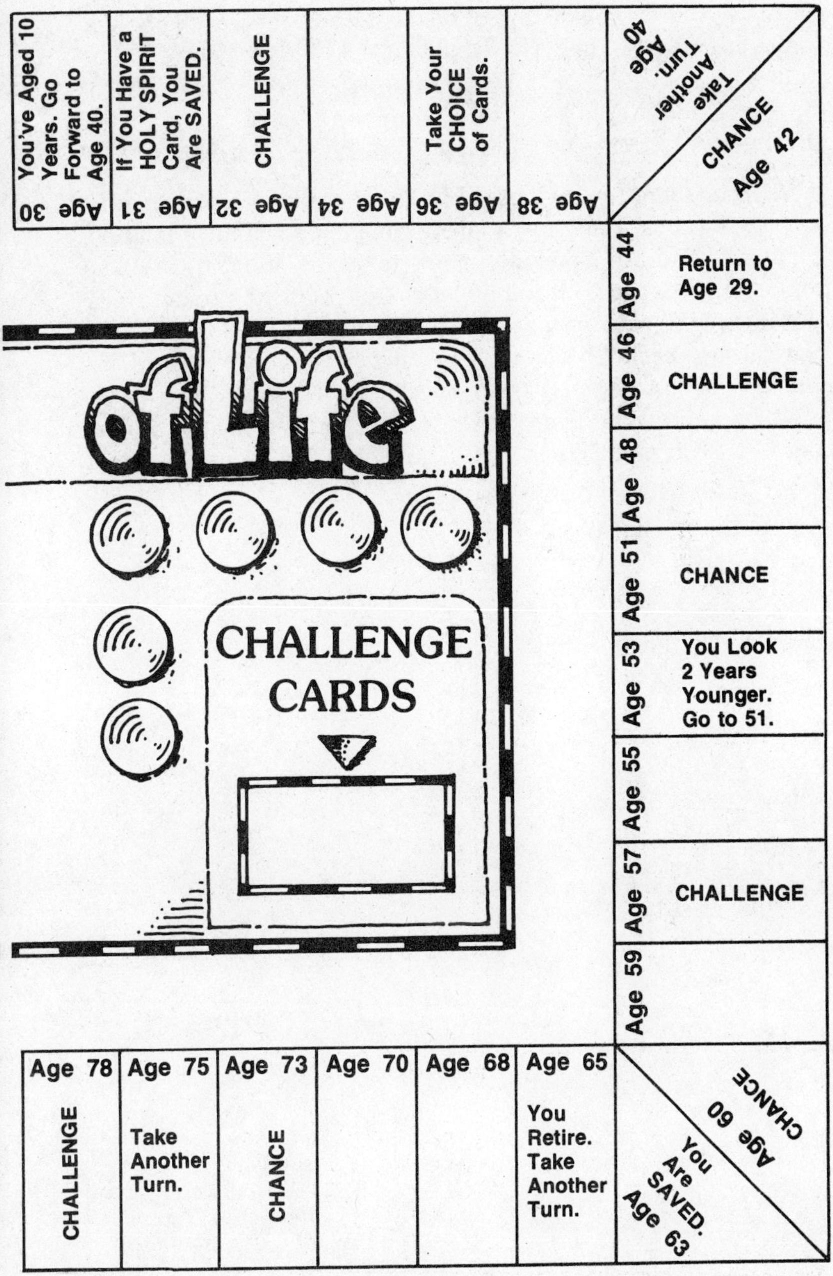

Age 30 You've Aged 10 Years. Go Forward to Age 40.
Age 31 If You Have a HOLY SPIRIT Card, You Are SAVED.
Age 32 CHALLENGE
Age 34
Age 36 Take Your CHOICE of Cards.
Age 38
Age 40 Take Another Turn.
Age 42 CHANCE
Age 44 Return to Age 29.
Age 46 CHALLENGE
Age 48
Age 51 CHANCE
Age 53 You Look 2 Years Younger. Go to 51.
Age 55
Age 57 CHALLENGE
Age 59
Age 60 CHANCE
Age 63 You Are SAVED.
Age 65 You Retire. Take Another Turn.
Age 68
Age 70
Age 73 CHANCE
Age 75 Take Another Turn.
Age 78 CHALLENGE
of Life
CHALLENGE CARDS

Chance Cards provide one of the best ways of obtaining Salvation in this Game of Life. Note that Chance Cards may be good or bad.

Challenge Cards

When you land on a CHALLENGE square, you are eligible to draw a Challenge Card. If you answer correctly, you may hold on to the card and use it—at any time—to add or subtract one year from your game life. This will be helpful to you if your token lands near any of the squares that offer Salvation (ages 20, 31, 63, 87). You can use each Challenge Card only once, and it is good for adding or subtracting only one year when you use it.

We have provided blank cards so that you can make up your own CHANCE and CHALLENGE cards to add to your fun in this game.

CHANCE	CHANCE	CHANCE
CHANCE	CHANCE	CHANCE
CHANCE	CHANCE	CHANCE
CHANCE	CHANCE	CHANCE
CHANCE	CHANCE	CHANCE
CHANCE	CHANCE	CHANCE
CHANCE	CHANCE	CHANCE

You became an alcoholic. Add 20 years to your life.	SALVATION You just asked Christ to save you!	ACCIDENT Ages 4-14: Add 4 years. Ages 16-25: Add 8 yrs. Ages 27-59: Add 11 yrs. Ages 60-up: You die!
Add or Subtract 2 years from your age.	SALVATION You are saved if you are between ages 4 and 22.	Return to age Sweet 16, if you are now 29 years old or less.
You've just aged 5 years.	You've had a face-lift. Subtract 3 years—at *any* time.	Roll the die and subract the number from your age.
HOLY SPIRIT CARD Hold on to this card: The Holy Spirit is working on you.	Your birth certificate has been lost. Return to age 10.	SALVATION Ages 4-25: You become a Christian if you have a Holy Spirit Card.
Add your real age to your game age.	You just *Died!*	SALVATION You are saved from sin *only* if you have a Holy Spirit Card.
Move to age 29.	You went into a coma and lost 5 years. Move ahead 5 years.	Subtract your real age from your game age.
ACCIDENT Ages 4-14: Add 1 year. Ages 16-25: Add 3 yrs. Ages 27-59: Add 5 yrs. Ages 60-up: Add 9 yrs.	ACCIDENT Ages 4-40: Add 2 years. Ages 42-59: Add 4 yrs. Ages 60-up: You die!	ACCIDENT Ages 16-25: You die! Ages 27-59: Add 5 yrs. Ages 60-up: Add 2 yrs.

CHALLENGE	CHALLENGE	CHALLENGE
CHALLENGE	CHALLENGE	CHALLENGE
CHALLENGE	CHALLENGE	CHALLENGE
CHALLENGE	CHALLENGE	CHALLENGE
CHALLENGE	CHALLENGE	CHALLENGE
CHALLENGE	CHALLENGE	CHALLENGE
CHALLENGE	CHALLENGE	CHALLENGE

There are many ways to heaven. True or False? John 14:6	What name is given by Peter as the way to heaven? Acts 4:11–12	What does John 3:16 say?
What have we done, as sheep do? Isaiah 53:6	We all have to die. After that comes what? Hebrews 9:27	You can never please God without what? Hebrews 11:6
What is a Christian? Romans 8:9–10	What two things do you have to do to be saved? Romans 10:9–10	Who is described in Luke 19:10 as the one who came to seek and to save the lost?
Whose sin was laid on Jesus? 2 Corinthians 5:20	A Christian should always be ready to do what? 1 Peter 3:15	Salvation is not a reward for what? Ephesians 2:9
If you believe in the Son of God, you may know what? 1 John 5:13	Our good works are worth what? Isaiah 64:6	What does Romans 3:23 say?
What does Jesus promise in John 10:10b?	**HOLY SPIRIT CARD** Hold on to this card. The Holy Spirit is working on you.	What does Romans 6:23 say?
If you believe in Jesus, what will you get? John 3:16	God doesn't want who to perish? 2 Peter 3:9	Christ died for us even when we were what? Romans 5:8